Designed by Father God
Text copyright © 2014 Dave Carroll
Illustrations copyright © 2014 Hannah Carroll & Elizabeth Carroll

Village House Press
Englewood, OH

ISBN: 978-1-6192795-2-0

All rights reserved. No part of this book may be reproduced or transmitted in any form or by any means, electronic or mechanical, including photocopying and recording, or by any information storage and retrieval system, without permission in writing from the author.

Unless otherwise indicated, all Bible quotations are taken from the *New American Standard Bible*®, Copyright © 1960, 1962, 1963, 1968, 1971, 1972, 1973, 1975, 1977, 1995 by The Lockman Foundation. Used by permission.

Scripture quotations marked (NIV) are taken from the Holy Bible, New International Version®, NIV®. Copyright © 1973, 1978, 1984, 2011 by Biblica, Inc.™ Used by permission of Zondervan. All rights reserved worldwide. www.zondervan.com The "NIV" and "New International Version" are trademarks registered in the United States Patent and Trademark Office by Biblica, Inc.™

DESIGNED by Father God

Written by Dave Carroll
Illustrated by Hannah and Elizabeth Carroll

Hi! My name is David, and these are my friends.
We love to do the things that most kids love to do.
We love to laugh. We love to sing.
And we love to dream about what our lives will be like when we grow up.

When people look at us, most of the time they only see our legs.
They only think about the things we are unable to do.
They think that we are not complete people,
that maybe we are this way because we are cursed,
or because God made a mistake,
or because someone in our family did something wrong.

But when we look at ourselves,
we don't wonder what other people think about us.

We ask, "What does **GOD** think about us?"

The Bible says that I wasn't a mistake at all.
I am a beautiful piece of artwork, designed carefully by God Himself.

*"For You formed my inward parts; You wove me in my mother's womb.
I will give thanks to You, for I am fearfully and wonderfully made."
Psalm 139:13-14*

I am not cursed. I am blessed! I am made in the image of God. When He designed me, God used Himself as a model!

"God created man in His own image, in the image of God He created him; male and female He created them."

Genesis 1:27-28

In fact, we were all designed to be like God and to live for Him.
But instead we chose to disobey God
because we wanted to live for ourselves.
The Bible calls that SIN.

The truth is, I am not the only one who has a problem.
The Bible says that EVERYBODY is born with sin...
and that's the biggest problem of all.

"For all have sinned and fall short of the glory of God."
Romans 3:23

But God is love, and because of His love,
He sent His Son Jesus to take the punishment for our sins.
He died so that we could be forgiven.
And God raised Him from the dead so that He could live in us.

Not because we did anything special to earn it,
but because God is a wonderful Father,
and because He loves us
and He wants us to be part of His family.

*"For God so loved the world
that He gave His only Son,
that whoever believes
in Him shall not perish,
but have eternal life."
John 3:16*

*"God demonstrates His own love toward us,
in that while we were yet sinners,
Christ died for us."
Romans 5:8*

He died for **ME**!
The only thing I have to do is to put my trust in Him.

"As many as received Him, to them He gave the right to become children of God, even to those who believe in His name."
John 1:12

That is amazing! God chose **ME** and adopted **ME** into His family!

"In love He predestined us to adoption as sons through Jesus Christ to Himself, according to the kind intention of His will."
Ephesians 1:4-5

I am a child of God. He loves me. God is my Father!

*"See how great a love the Father has bestowed on us,
that we would be called children of God."*
1 John 3:1

He can do anything and He knows everything.

"Great is our Lord and abundant in strength; His understanding is infinite."
Psalm 147:5

He always does what is right.

"His work is perfect, for all His ways are just; a God of faithfulness and without injustice, righteous and upright is He."
Deuteronomy 32:4

He knows everything about me.

"O Lord, You have searched me and known me. You know when I sit down and when I rise up; You understand my thought from afar...and are intimately acquainted with all my ways. Even before there is a word on my tongue, behold, O Lord, You know it all."
Psalm 139:1-4

He is always watching over me.

"He will not allow your foot to slip; He who keeps you will not slumber. The Lord will guard your going out and your coming in from this time forth and forever."
Psalm 121:3, 8

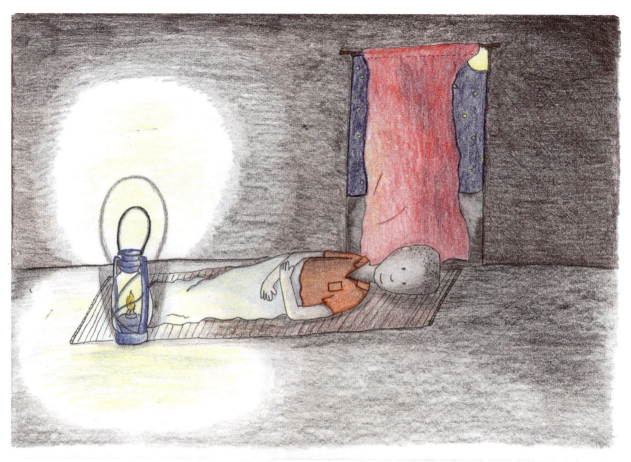

He could never forget about me.

"Can a woman forget her nursing child and have no compassion on the son of her womb? Even these may forget, but I will not forget you. Behold, I have inscribed you on the palms of My hands."
Isaiah 49:15-16

In fact, He thinks about me so much that the Bible says
it would be impossible to count His thoughts about me!

*"How precious also are Your thoughts to me, O God! How vast is the sum of them!
If I should count them, they would outnumber the sand."*
Psalm 139:17-18

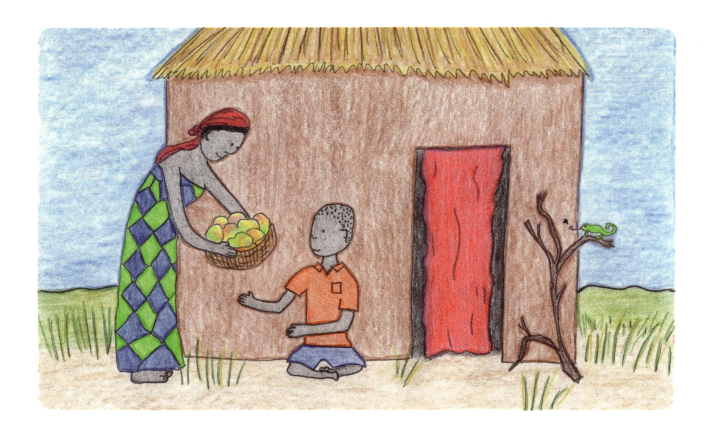

He cares about all of my fears and worries, and He knows everything that I need, even before I ask Him.

"Do not worry then, saying, 'What will we eat?' or 'What will we drink?' or 'What will we wear for clothing?' For your heavenly Father knows that you need all these things."
Matthew 6:31-32

He is my friend. I can talk to Him anytime!

"The Lord hears when I call to Him."
Psalm 4:3

He will NEVER abandon me. I don't have to worry that He will ever send me away. He is my Father, and the Bible says He will remind me every day, so that I can always know for certain that I am His child!

"The Spirit Himself testifies with our spirit that we are children of God."
Romans 8:16

And nothing could ever take His love away from me.

"For I am convinced that neither death, nor life, nor angels, nor principalities, nor things present, nor things to come, nor powers, nor height, nor depth, nor any other created thing will be able to separate us from the love of God, which is in Christ Jesus or Lord."
Romans 8:38-39

My Father has great plans for me. I am not useless, because He gives me everything I need to do the things that He has called me to do.

"For we are His workmanship, created in Christ Jesus for good works, which God prepared beforehand so that we would walk in them."
Ephesians 2:10

He can use me to tell people about Him
and to show them how wonderful He is!

"You will receive power when the Holy Spirit has come upon you; and you shall be My witnesses."
Acts 1:8

He has given me special gifts and abilities to serve Him.

"As each one has received a special gift, employ it in serving one another as good stewards of the manifold grace of God."
1 Peter 4:10

He can do things through me that I can't even imagine.

"Now to Him who is able to do far more abundantly beyond all that we ask or think, according to the power that works within us, to Him be the glory."
Ephesians 3:20-21

I have HIS power working in me. He makes me strong!

"Most gladly, therefore, I will rather boast about my weaknesses, so that the power of Christ may dwell in me...for when I am weak, then I am strong."
2 Corinthians 12:9-10

I am not limited at all…In Him, I am COMPLETE!

"And in Him you have been made complete."
Colossians 2:10

I have been perfectly designed by a perfect Father.
And no matter what anyone else thinks or says about me,
I know that I am more valuable than anything in the world...
because I am a child of GOD!
Just being with Him makes me happy!

"In Your presence is fullness of joy"
Psalm 16:11

And just being with me makes **HIM** happy!

"He will take great delight in you, He will quiet you with His love, He will rejoice over you with singing."
Zephaniah 3:17 (NIV)

It makes Him so happy that He is preparing a special place for me, so that I can go and be with Him.

"In My Father's house are many dwelling places...I go to prepare a place for you. If I go and prepare a place for you, I will come again and receive you to Myself, that where I am, there you may be also."
John 14:2-3

I'm going to live with my Father in heaven...forever.
It's going to be wonderful!

"And I heard a loud voice from the throne, saying, 'Behold, the tabernacle of God is among men, and He will dwell among them, and they shall be His people, and God Himself will be among them, and He will wipe away every tear from their eyes; and there will no longer be any death; there will no longer be any mourning, or crying, or pain. And He who sits on the throne said, 'Behold, I am making all things new.'"
Revelation 21:3-5

About the Author and Illustrators

Dave Carroll has been a missionary in Uganda since 1997. He currently serves as the director of Revolutionary Love Ministries. His passion is to lead people into a life-transforming understanding of God as their Father through the love of Christ. He loves to teach the depths and the beauty of God's word and to share his life with young people who have never experienced real fatherhood. Dave lives in Uganda with his wife, Jen, and their four children.

Hannah and Elizabeth Carroll are not only sisters, but also best friends. They have spent most of their lives in Uganda and they love sharing life and being involved in ministry with their family. They both have a calling to serve the Lord as missionaries and a desire to use their gifts and creativity to share the love of Christ with as many people as possible.